T0015032

PRAYING MANTIS VS. BLACK WIDOW SPIDER

BY KIERAN DOWNS

BELLWETHER MEDIA · MINNEAPOLIS, MN

Torque brims with excitement
perfect for thrill-seekers of all kinds.
Discover daring survival skills, explore
uncharted worlds, and marvel at mighty
engines and extreme sports. In *Torque* books,
anything can happen. Are you ready?

This edition first published in 2022 by Bellwether Media, Inc.

No part of this publication may be reproduced in whole or in part without
written permission of the publisher. For information regarding permission,
write to Bellwether Media, Inc., Attention: Permissions Department,
6012 Blue Circle Drive, Minnetonka, MN 55343.

Library of Congress Cataloging-in-Publication Data

Names: Downs, Kieran, author.
Title: Praying mantis vs. black widow spider / by Kieran Downs.
Other titles: Praying mantis versus black widow spider
Description: Minneapolis, MN : Bellwether Media, Inc., 2022. | Series:
   Torque: animal battles | Includes bibliographical references and index.
   | Audience: Ages 7-12 | Audience: Grades 3-7 | Summary: "Amazing
   photography accompanies engaging information about the fighting
   abilities of praying mantises and black widow spiders. The combination
   of high-interest subject matter and light text is intended for students
   in grades 3 through 7" – Provided by publisher.
Identifiers: LCCN 2021039734 (print) | LCCN 2021039735 (ebook) | ISBN
   9781644876251 (library binding) | ISBN 9781648346880 (paperback) |
   ISBN 9781648346361 (ebook)
Subjects: LCSH: Praying mantis–Juvenile literature. | Black widow
   spider–Juvenile literature.
Classification: LCC QL505.9.M35 D69 2022 (print) | LCC QL505.9.M35
   (ebook) | DDC 595.7/27–dc23
LC record available at https://lccn.loc.gov/2021039734
LC ebook record available at https://lccn.loc.gov/2021039735

Editor: Rebecca Sabelko   Designer: Josh Brink

Printed in the United States of America, North Mankato, MN.

TABLE OF CONTENTS

THE COMPETITORS

In the animal kingdom, even small animals can be dangerous. Praying mantises are **vicious** hunters. They surprise **prey** with powerful attacks at super speeds.

But praying mantises are not the only small animals that do damage. Black widow spiders knock out prey with their deadly **venom**. Who would win in a battle between these **carnivores**?

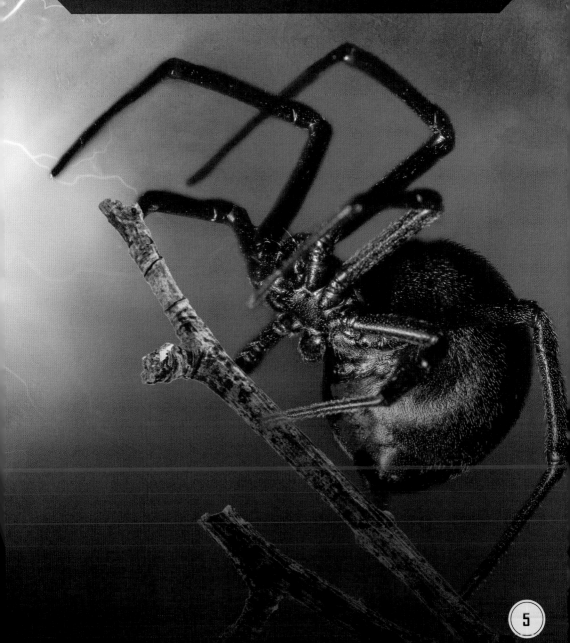

EUROPEAN PRAYING MANTIS PROFILE

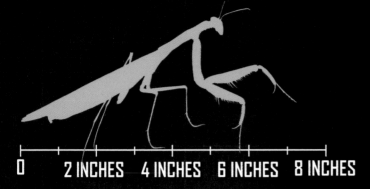

0   2 INCHES   4 INCHES   6 INCHES   8 INCHES

LENGTH
UP TO 6 INCHES
(15.2 CENTIMETERS)

WEIGHT
AROUND .18 OUNCES
(5 GRAMS)

HABITAT

SAVANNAS   SHRUBLANDS   GRASSLANDS   DESERTS

EUROPEAN PRAYING MANTIS RANGE

RANGE

EATING MATES

Female praying mantises are known for eating their mates. When they do this, females lay twice as many eggs as they usually would.

Praying mantises are **insects** with triangle-shaped heads. Their long, bent front legs make it look like they are praying. These hunters use their long legs to grab onto insects, frogs, and other prey.

There are more than 1,800 different **species** of praying mantis. Many have brown or green bodies. Their colors help them hide among plants.

Black widow spiders are **arachnids**. They spin strong webs in dry, dark places. They use their webs to catch food.

Black widows are black or gray. Females have red **hourglass** markings on their bellies. Males are smaller than females. They sometimes have markings on their bellies, too.

MALE BLACK WIDOW SPIDER

FEMALE BLACK WIDOW SPIDER

SOUTHERN BLACK WIDOW PROFILE

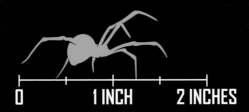

0   1 INCH   2 INCHES

LENGTH
UP TO 0.5 INCHES
(1.3 CENTIMETERS)

WEIGHT
UP TO .04 OUNCES
(1.1 GRAMS)

HABITAT

DESERTS   FORESTS   RAIN FORESTS   GRASSLANDS

SOUTHERN BLACK WIDOW RANGE

■ RANGE

SECRET WEAPONS

Black widows spin webs of sticky silk. Some threads are made to catch prey. When animals stick to these threads, one end releases. Prey falls into the web!

200°

360°

HUMAN: 200 DEGREES   PRAYING MANTIS: 360 DEGREES

Praying mantises are the only insects whose eyes can see **depth**. They can also see in all directions. Their eyes help them know when to strike their prey.

Praying mantises have long front legs. They quickly **extend** these legs to catch prey. They snatch flying insects out of the air!

NOT MUCH VENOM

Black widows' venom can be harmful to humans. But they rarely deliver enough venom to kill people.

1 INCH

0

BLACK WIDOW FANG
ABOUT 0.04 INCHES (1 MILLIMETER)

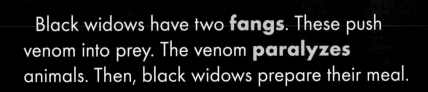

Black widows have two **fangs**. These push venom into prey. The venom **paralyzes** animals. Then, black widows prepare their meal.

EYES

LONG FRONT LEGS

LEG SPIKES

Sharp spikes line the front legs of praying mantises. The spikes are used to catch prey. Mantises use their back legs to pin animals down.

BLACK WIDOW

STICKY WEBS

FANGS

LEG HAIRS

Black widows have small hairs on their legs. They use these to wrap their prey in silk. Then, their food is ready to eat.

ATTACK MOVES

Praying mantises are **ambush hunters**. They blend in with surrounding plants while they wait for prey.

Spiders set traps in their webs. Then, they hang upside down to wait for prey. Webs **vibrate** when animals get stuck. When black widows feel the movement, they attack!

MANTIS MEALS

Praying mantises sometimes eat small birds. In some cases, they eat birds' brains!

Once the prey is close, praying mantises strike. Their front legs spring forward to grab prey. The mantises eat their captured meal headfirst.

Black widows bite their prey many times. They push a special **substance** into the animal. It turns their insides into liquid. Then, the spiders suck out their meal!

READY, FIGHT!

A black widow starts to spin its web. But a praying mantis is hiding nearby. When the black widow comes close, the mantis attacks!

The mantis grabs the spider with its sharp spikes. The spider tries to bite with its fangs. But it cannot reach far enough. The mantis found its meal!

GLOSSARY

ambush hunters—animals that sit and wait to catch their prey

arachnids—animals with two body segments and four pairs of legs

carnivores—animals that eat only meat

depth—how far away something is

extend—to stretch out

fangs—long, pointed teeth

hourglass—related to a tool used for measuring time; the top and bottom of an hourglass are wide while the middle is thin.

insects—small animals with six legs and hard outer bodies; an insect's body is divided into three parts.

paralyzes—makes unable to move

prey—animals that are hunted by other animals for food

species—kinds of animals

substance—a certain kind of material

venom—a poison made by black widow spiders

vibrate—to move back and forth rapidly

vicious—dangerously violent

TO LEARN MORE

AT THE LIBRARY

Adamson, Thomas K. *Scorpion vs. Tarantula*. Minneapolis, Minn.: Bellwether Media, 2021.

Culliford, Amy. *Black Widow Spider*. New York, N.Y.: Crabtree Publishing, 2022.

Mone, Gregory. *Strange Nature: The Insect Portraits of Levon Biss*. New York, N.Y.: Abrams Books for Young Readers, 2021.

ON THE WEB

FACTSURFER

Factsurfer.com gives you a safe, fun way to find more information.

1. Go to www.factsurfer.com

2. Enter "praying mantis vs. black widow spider" into the search box and click 🔍.

3. Select your book cover to see a list of related content.

INDEX

The images in this book are reproduced through the courtesy of: Ara Rahman, front cover (praying mantis head); Evgeniy Ayupov, front cover (praying mantis body); Ernest Cooper/ Alamy, front cover (black widow spider); Kristina Postnikova, pp. 2-3, 14, 20-24 (praying mantis); Jay Ondreicka, pp. 2-3, 20-24 (black widow spider); Lutsenko Olekandr, p. 4; Jacobo Queo, p. 5; Cornel Constantin, pp. 6-7; Mark_Kostich, pp. 8-9, 15 (stick webs); jjpoole, pp. 10, 15 (fangs); tea maeklong, p. 11; Chris Moody, p. 12; Pong Wira, p. 13; Paul Looyen, p. 14 (eyes); Detyukov Sergey, p. 14 (long front legs); Apurv Jadhav, p. 14 (leg spikes); Therina Groenewald, p. 15; Phil Degginger/ Alamy, p. 15 (leg hairs); Ava Peattie, p. 16; Scott Camazine/ Alamy, p. 17; Robert Keresztes, p. 18; EdwardSnow, p. 19.